ALL IN DIVINE ORDER

NOTHING HAPPENS BY ACCIDENT!

DR. MONICA YOUNG ANDREWS

TABLE OF CONTENTS

All In Divine Order	v
Acknowledgments	vii
Preface	xi
The Divine Order Foundation	1
Chapter 1 - My Story	3
Chapter 2 - Relationships and Health	11
Chapter 3 - Grandma Helen	17
Chapter 4 - Daddy	21
Chapter 5 - Mentors for a Reason, a Season, a Lifetime	25
Chapter 6 - Apollo the Dog	31
Chapter 7 - Partners in Shine	36
Call to Action	39
About the Author	41

ALL IN DIVINE ORDER
NOTHING HAPPENS BY ACCIDENT!

Dr. Monica Young Andrews

Copyright © 2020 – Dr. Monica Young Andrews

All rights reserved. This book is protected by the copyright laws of the United States of America. This book may not be copied or reprinted for commercial gain or profit. The use of quotations or occasional page copying for personal or group study is permitted and encouraged. Permission will be granted upon request.

Soft cover ISBN: 978-1-7355168-0-6

Library of Congress Cataloging-in-Publication Data

Names: Andrews, Dr. Monica Young

Title: All In Divine Order: Nothing Happens by Accident! /

Library of Congress Control Number: 2020917437

Dr. Monica Young Andrews / Divine Order

Perry Hall, Maryland 21128

www.divineordernetwork.com

Original Cover Photo by De'Vaughn Jenkins

Proceeds donated to Divine Order Foundation

Perry Hall, Maryland

ACKNOWLEDGMENTS

This book is respectfully dedicated to those in my life, young and seasoned, who have been placed somewhere in the divine order of my fifty-plus-year journey. First and foremost, my Heavenly Father God, my Lord and Savior Jesus Christ, and my Holy Spirit, who have always provided and continue to provide me with the true experiences of divine order, allowing my faith to tremendously surpass all understanding; my beloved Mum and Daddy, Rose Thurston and the late Walter M. Young; grandmothers, the late Florence Jones, the late Helen Young, and Gwendolyn Andrews; my amazing gifts, De'Vaughn Jenkins and his son, Isaiah Jenkins; my husband and soulmate, Sean Andrews; my late sister, Valerie Young; my baby sister, Rachelle Roberts; my "family forever," Vincent Jenkins; my "first baby," Juana Jenkins; my other "babies," Jordan and Lauren Andrews; my beautiful, special niece, Kayla Simone Roberts; my awesome grands, Jahmir, Naiya, and Taylor Redmond; my late godson, Kelvin Smallwood Jones; my uncle, Joseph Young; my Aunts, Ruth Coward, Thelma Garner, Yvonne Young Woodson, and the late Marie Thompson; my cousins, the late Bryson Ambrose Young, Brian and Katie

Young, Brandilyn Young, Corey and Erin Coward, Cynthia Thompson Scott, Yvette Thompson, Andrea Fletcher, Michael Young, Nancy Young, Theresa Young, Carolyn Young, Arleen and James Jeter, Paul Thompson, Anthony Thompson, Joanne Gould, Regina Alvarez, Mia Orantes, Sunil Gupta, the late Veronica "Roni" DJ Sermons, Tonnett Brooks, Darryle Brooks, and Renee Clifford; my late stepmother, Carolyn Young Bothuel; the best mother-in-law ever, Lauren P. Andrews, Lorraine Lansey, and Donald Spellman; all of those whom God has allowed to participate in some form or fashion in my divine order: my brothers, Reynaldo and Mykel Thurston; my nephew, Thomas Thurston; Jeffrey Grant, Antoini Jones, Lucy Jones, Terrie Howard Carter, Rhonda Leach Lewis, Natasha Nickens Driggers, Paulette Clark, Gina Smallwood Jones, Lisa Ratcliff Cross, Kimberly Brackett Brooks, Tahira Murphy, Jameelah Richardson, Cheryl Hartfield, Leonet Outlaw, Deborah and Dominique White, Pamela Cousins, Samirah Brown, Alphonso and Michell Brooks, Carl Merriweather, Paul Miles, Byron Hall, Donald and Angela Williams, Cindy Taylor Little, Alicia 'Penny' Brown, Donald 'Doc' Smith, Melanie Lewis, Derrick and Natalie Smith, Corey McDowell, Latasha Rozier-Behlin, Audranette Arrington, Garry Jones, Alphonso Wilkerson, Felicia Cooper-Lyles, Dee Spraker, Charles and Andrea Jenkins, Theirrien "Tee" Clark and Marcy Myles-Clark, Jessie and Vanity James, Michael Taylor, Michael Lewis, Mary McGill, Morganai Kelley, Vanessa Miller Fuentes, Judith Bowman Howie Banks, Dr. Bruce and Bernice McClure, Pamela Sinclair, Arnette Riddick, Wendy Williams Golston, Gary Tatum, Mary McLean, Angela and Michael Neal, Edwin McClure, Rick and Patsy Adsit, Todd and Alex Dildine,

Dave and Dionne Mitchell, Maxine Adams, Susan Priest, Kelly Thomas, Donald Bradley, Mike and Gayle Toloff, Parimal and Jennifer Naik, Sue Griffin, Pat Karas, Nicola Smith Jackson, Robert Jackson, Sandy Amerman, Gregg and Frenita Amerman, Chuck Pereira, Barry and Rose Menser, Price Wilkes, Soda, Thomas Harrelson, Macarthur Seaberry, Lawrence 'LT' Turner, Dr. Amanda Carter, Ashely Boston, Tiffany Hill, Ricardo Daniels, William Mark Waddell, the late Tyrone Thomas, Kim Whitmon, Vash and Jamila Johnson, Kay and Marc Miller, Elaine Rosenberg, Sharonne Jackson-Little, Janice McLean, Phylecia Persaud, Janice Farmer, Janice Wilbourn, Trina Palmore, Mike and Lorna Miller, Randy and Michelle Donnell, Dr. Michael Roberts, Dr. Tamika Anderson, Tanise Anderson, Roger and Cheryl Grant, Aanand Shukla, Todd and Azuree Dalton, Tyrone Allen, Arnetta Cobb Carter Wilson, Dr. Jerome and Dr. Arlene Spann, Dr. James Wilkerson, Dr. Eve Taylor, Dr. Morris Redd, Peter Voogd, Austin Netzley, Coach Kim McDaniel, Dr. Willis Eubanks, Dr. Diane Moore-Eubanks, Cairo, Dakar and Sudan Eubanks, and the GODSU family; Jonathan Green, the Godsend without whom I could not have completed this work in its current form; and every God-breathed person around the world who embraces or needs to embrace their divine order in their purposeful life... This includes YOU!

PREFACE

I decided to write this book as a way to honor my cousin, Bryson Ambrose Young, who died at the tender age of twenty. On August 4, 1994, he entered this world at a whopping five pounds. At such a low birth weight, doctors weren't even sure if he was going to survive. But he did, and he spent every day of his life overcoming the obstacles he faced. He was intelligent, popular, and outgoing, and he was an African American child who not only loved Spanish but spoke it better than a lot of native Spanish speakers.

On June 28, 2015, he slipped away in his sleep. There were no known medical issues, other than a slightly enlarged heart, and the preliminary autopsy showed no signs of foul play. Yet, how many twenty-year-old people do you know who go to sleep and don't wake up in the morning? We were all in shock, and we spent months waiting for the final autopsy results.

I want you to understand how important it is to live life to the fullest. My family has spent so much of its time in the shadow of death. I'm the oldest child of three, and my middle sister was born with sickle cell anemia, a gene that both of my parents carry. She was only ten months younger than me and died eight days before her thirtieth birthday. After she died, I learned that her doctors never thought that she would make it past her teens, but she more than doubled what they initially expected for someone with her condition. Instead of seeing her life as a tragedy, we should see it as a great success because she overcame her obstacles.

Having somebody so close to you in your life one day and gone the next shows you the urgency of living according to your goals and dreams – Your Purpose – and I passed that value down to my son. After being away from home for a week or so, he discovered his passion and announced that he wanted to fly airplanes. With no training, he was ready to give up a college education, for which we'd spent his entire life planning. But I could hear the determination in his voice and became determined to find a way for him to accomplish his new goal.

Because I'm big on personal development, I am very familiar with the book "Think and Grow Rich" by Napoleon Hill, and I am a fan of Les Brown. With their words in my mind, I instructed my son to visit the local airport not far from our house every day. He was to let them know his passion for wanting to fly and ask if he could work there. Even if they said no, he should still show up and help out wherever he could (without pay) until they hired him.

Well, it worked because he worked it! I was proud that my son showed up to that airport EVERY DAY and stayed until it shut down. They eventually hired him, and before he was twenty years old, he was teaching others to fly while still learning more flying skills. My grandmother, who we call Gee-Gee, used her own savings to help him accelerate through his courses to become a pilot.

There are plenty of doubters in this world. My son had a rough time growing up and made some poor decisions when he was younger. Most of us made bad decisions when we were children, but there's a huge difference between the decisions we make as children and as adults. Who am I to judge someone based on what they did when they were twelve? Even more importantly, who am I to stop someone from achieving their dreams?

After what happened with my sister and my nephew, I truly believe that life can be short. And if you're reading this, I want you to grab the same sense of passion and urgency when you chase your dreams! As the great Bard said in his amazing play, *Henry V*, "Tonight, eat, drink, and be merry, for tomorrow we die." That's how I want you to live your life – not with the fear of death looming over you, but living in the moment so that, when death does come for you, you will have no regrets. You can say that you've lived your life following your path, all in divine order.

When people hear the story of my son becoming a pilot, most of them think, "That sounds great, but my family could never afford to train someone to be a pilot. We don't have the money, and we're not in a situation to create those opportunities."

I want you to know that there are a lot of ways to make things happen, and I am going to share some of them with you. Just read on!

THE DIVINE ORDER FOUNDATION

The Divine Order Foundation, a Private Family Foundation, was started to elevate the spirnancial well-being of humanity, one person, family, community, company at a time, through education, tools, and experience. You may be saying, "Spirnancial? Never heard that word before. What's that?" Spirnancial is a word God put on my heart that simply means spiritual-mental-emotional-physical-social-financial, in that order. At some point, you'll probably even see variations of spirnancial (Spirnancially, spirnance, spirnancing, etc.) in the dictionary.

Through the Divine Order Foundation, we support, participate in and complete different projects assisting and uplifting humanity, with a focus on seniors, veterans and, of course, the youth in our community – our future – to achieve their dreams, unlock their potential and move into their God-given purpose.

To help my son become a pilot, I had to rely on the help of others, but Gee-Gee was always there, cheering for us. Despite all of these challenges, we still have other members in our family who have health and medical problems and short lifespans, and we do everything we can to live an amazing life with the amount of time that God has given us on this earth.

Because you never know how much time you have, you want to live every day feeling fulfilled and full of passion as you travel the path to your dreams and your purpose so that you have no regrets.

It's not easy to run a foundation. You want to do your best, but there are so many people that need help. We are not just throwing money at the people who ask. We have a whole process to help people demonstrate that they are on the path to success, that they're trying to achieve their dreams, and that there will be an amazing return on investment.

As much as money can help, passion is just as important. That's why we want to teach you how to unlock your passion and purpose. When you do, the rest of your plan will fall together, and you will discover the divine order in your own life.

Gee-Gee and I want people to take affirmative action. There's money out there for those who are willing to put their heads down, meet us halfway and pay for their part of the equity with the sweat of their brow.

The Gee-Gee Scholarship is being established to bless those youth who have found their passion but lack the finances to make it happen. To donate to the Gee-Gee Scholarship fund, please visit www.divineordernetwork.com, where you'll find the donate button.

CHAPTER 1 - MY STORY

And we know that all things work together for good to those who love God, to those who are called according to His purpose.
– Romans 8:28 NKJV

MY JOURNEY BEGAN with a trip to church. One night, I came home after partying in a club and having a good time with my friends. I can't remember exactly what time it was, but my mother caught me on the way to bed and shouted at me, "You're going to get up tomorrow and go to church, period. You live in my house; you're going to church."

I grew up Catholic, and I never felt like I was getting anything out of it. I was just showing up and going through the motions. While Catholicism is reverently ritualistic and traditional, I had a lot of questions, and the answers didn't make sense to me. We had to kneel, sit, stand, and follow the songs, just blindly doing what they wanted us to do during mass. I was following a set of instructions, but I didn't feel an emotional closeness to the Lord while doing these things.

My father understood what I meant by not feeling a connection with the Catholic church. He, too, grew up Catholic but eventually joined a different worship group. He once told me, "Whatever you do, don't rob God because of man. Give God His time by visiting other worship places until you find where you're supposed to be. Every weekend, whether it's Baptist, AME, Muslim, Jehovah's witness, etc., get up and go somewhere to give God His time." I didn't have to go to a Catholic church, but I needed to find somewhere where I could connect with God and a congregation.

So, on that particular day, instead of sitting there and waiting to go with my mother, I grabbed my baby sister, and we went to mass together.

We wound up at the Franciscan Monastery of the Holy Land in America, where they had beautiful grounds, complete with replicas of prisons and ruins from the Holy Land. My favorite part about that church was that early morning masses were quite short (20-30 minutes maximum). That day, we sat, stood, kneeled, and stood again, following the usual pattern, until I blacked out for the first time in my life.

At that point, I had been going through a lifelong issue with sleeping. I would often go for several days without sleeping. That day, I had spent a couple of days awake, partying and living on the edge. People would always wonder how I could do it and where I got all the energy. I would sometimes say to them, "I'll get my sleep when I get to heaven." But that day, I wasn't in heaven; I was in church. And for a few brief moments, I "fell asleep" standing up in front of everybody. My sister had to tug on my arm before I came to and sat down.

Fortunately, I was able to make it back home and go straight to sleep. **At that moment, when every-**

thing faded to black, I learned that you can only push yourself so far. God will always tell you when it's time to make a change – when you've danced a little too close to the fire and need to change your life, sooner rather than later.

That was the first time I felt a sign from God that I was headed in the wrong direction. But it wasn't the last.

I WENT to Hampton Institute (now Hampton University) in Virginia. One summer morning, home from school, I was on my way to my summer job. I had a green light and was only driving twenty-five or thirty miles an hour when someone ran the red light, hitting me head-on and causing me to spin several times until I hit the dent of a lamp post. Fortunately, they struck me from the right side of the car, and I had no passengers. As I looked over at the seat next to me, glaring at the passenger door almost kissing the console, I knew that if somebody had been sitting there, they would not have walked away from that accident.

I finished my schooling at Hampton in December 1987 and walked in the spring of 1988. After my graduation in May, I was not looking to stay with my mother; we just had too much strife in the house. That painful accident turned into a blessing in disguise because it put me in a good financial situation. I ended up buying a house half-a-block away from where I grew up in Northeast Washington, District of Columbia (DC). I could even see my old bedroom windows from my new house. I spent that summer fixing everything up, and I was really proud of what I'd accomplished.

The tragedy that struck me – an accident that

could have killed me – made me realize that I needed a change in my life. When unexpected things happen to us, whether they be good or bad, we should always look beyond the event itself to discover what it really means. As I learned early on, it's all in Divine Order!

A YEAR LATER, my cousin moved in with me. In July 1989, she was going out with her friends one night to celebrate her birthday and wanted me to go with her. I didn't want to go because my hair wasn't done, and I wasn't feeling sociable. But she kept prodding and insisting until I finally gave in. So, I put on a hat, slipped on an outfit, and headed out the door.

That's when I met who was to become my first husband. Four months later, he proposed, and we got married. Unfortunately, the relationship didn't have a happily ever after, and we separated. He was struggling with some addiction problems, and I had problems of my own and just couldn't have someone with those problems living with me, especially after our son was born in 1991.

My son is the best thing that has ever happened to me, and it happened because I decided to not care about my hair or my feelings and just make my cousin happy.

THE ONLY TIME I've ever been pregnant was when I was pregnant with my son. I've never been in a situation in which I had to terminate a pregnancy because I was not ready for it. That's a tough situation that many young women go through, and I made a conscious decision that I would never let it happen to me.

ALL IN DIVINE ORDER 7

From the age of seventeen, I decided to be "mature" about my procreation decisions and started taking birth control pills. While they kept me from becoming pregnant, they also had the side effect of destroying my uterus by growing fibroids. And because the fibroids had grown for such a long time, I had to have an emergency hysterectomy in 2000.

Sometimes, we think we're doing the right thing, like taking those pills and trying to be a responsible adult. But we may end up hurting ourselves because we don't know all of the side effects, we haven't been told all of the information, or we make the choice not to follow what God says about sex outside of marriage. Every decision has its consequences.

IN THE MID-1990S, my first hubby and I divorced. Back then, in DC, if you needed to refinance your home but your spouse wasn't on the mortgage or deed, they still needed to show up at the closing to sign their rights away. I didn't want to have to locate him whenever I needed to get something done, so he signed the divorce papers uncontested. As I casually took the papers to court to file, I didn't carry the divorce on my shoulders; not many even knew about it.

He and I would go back and forth between living together and separating over the course of nineteen years. I've always said that I'd never fight another woman for any man, yet I ended up fighting an addiction for my husband. I'm not sure which is worse, but I do know that the experience was one of the best ways to expose my codependent role in enabling his addiction.

I will never forget my cousin Roni, who had me read the book *Women Who Love Too Much* by Robin

Norwood. That book changed my life! To this day, I highly recommend it to anyone struggling with codependency.

When my son graduated from catholic school in the eighth grade, he had an outburst and just lost it. Although he had decent grades, he was constantly getting in trouble, and I had a feeling that high school wouldn't be any better.

In his ninth-grade year, we ended up putting him in a small but expensive private school with an average class size of just five students. I had to take out a loan on my house to create this opportunity for my son to give him the time he needed. It was a very challenging time for me to risk my home, and unfortunately, it didn't work out. I put almost everything on the line, but it still wasn't enough.

When our son was near the end of the ninth grade, we all moved to Glenn Dale, Maryland. We had more space, but I was still concerned about him. We had taken him away from his friends, his home, and everything he knew. I thought we were giving him a more comfortable home and more opportunities, but it just seemed to throw everything out of balance.

He went to the neighborhood public school in the tenth grade. His daddy and I were not doing well and couldn't agree on how to handle him. I was getting more upset with both of them every day. Eventually, I left for months and didn't come back until I realized that I was still paying the mortgage as well as someone else to stay with them. When I told him that I was coming back and he had to go, he and my son left.

Meanwhile, my son kept having problems at school. We talked to the school, to the doctors, to the church, and even to the local authorities to find out what we could do to help him. They all had similar responses. "Nothing, except put him on medication," or "Nothing, until he's in the penal system," or "Nothing. It's up to him," or "There's nothing anybody can do."

Eventually, we took him to a clinic called the Amen Clinic with Dr. Daniel Amen in Virginia. We were blessed to be able to drive, as people fly from all over the country to be tested there. They did brain scans and multiple tests for things I didn't entirely understand, but I understood them much better than his psychological results. In the end, it turned out that my son had ADD. They were able to isolate which stage of the ADD process he was in and figure out what was causing him to engage in risky or dangerous behaviors.

The very thing that caused my son to be such a challenging student when he was younger was the same thing that gives him a thrill when he flies planes now. All we needed to do was figure out how to channel his energy into something about which he was passionate. When my son decided he wanted to be a pilot, that unlocked his future and changed his life forever. All in Divine Order!

Reflection Questions

1. Have you ever pushed yourself so hard that you forgot what you were meant to be doing?

2. Have you ever sacrificed long-term success for something in the short term?

3. Do you sometimes have to learn the hard way? Do you only start making changes when something drastic happens?

4. Have you been changed by a tragedy, only to realize later that the change didn't last?

5. How does it feel when something unexpected but amazing happens?

6. Often, one little decision can change the course of your life. How does that make you feel?

7. Have you ever struggled to find the right path for your life or your children's lives?

8. Have you ever recognized events in your life that you knew were all in divine order?

Activities

This book is meant to inspire and guide you. Some inspiration will hopefully come from the personal stories I'm sharing with you, but the guiding requires a little action on your part. We learn from reading, but we only change when we take action. To start on the path to success, start tracking your own journey. Go out today and buy a journal that you can fill with your stories, hopes, and dreams – a place to reflect, be yourself, and find your own path. If you're the type who doesn't like to write, go to your app store and download a journal app so that you can record yourself speaking instead of writing. Whatever you choose to do, I encourage you to do it today!

The reflection questions included within each chapter are a great jumping-off point for your first few journal entries. It's helpful to have a place where you can express yourself without external influence – where you can delve into what you really want from life. Once you truly understand what you want, that dream becomes achievable.

CHAPTER 2 - RELATIONSHIPS AND HEALTH

My brethren, count it all joy when you fall into various trials, knowing that the testing of your faith produces patience. But let patience have its perfect work, that you may be perfect and complete, lacking nothing. If any of you lacks wisdom, let him ask of God, who gives to all liberally and without reproach, and it will be given to him.

– James 1:2-5 NKJV

I ALWAYS TELL PEOPLE, "Make a list as you're recovering from a breakup. Take some time to reflect and get to know yourself. Write out the things you loved about that relationship and the things you didn't."

That's one of the things I learned to do in counseling. As a matter of fact, I took it to a whole other level and started my list with two columns: "**Must Have**" and "**Must Not Have.**" I wrote traits under each column as they came to me, even going back to prior relationships that I hadn't considered before.

When I went back to the dating scene, I could spot the red flags a lot easier because of that list. You see, we are emotional beings, and I knew that my emotions could cloud the facts, which is why I referenced my lists many times during this dating journey. Eventually, I added a third column, "**Can Bend.**" My list was ever-evolving. After each experience I had, I'd add new traits to each column and switch old traits from **Can Bend** to **Must Have** or **Must Not Have**. This list contributed to my growth and evolution.

Once you reach a certain age, you just don't have time to waste. One thing I caution about your list is this: whoever you're dating needs to already bring to the table the "Must Have" and "Must Not Have" traits. It's not for you to teach them. If you think you might be teaching them, you'll end up realizing that they were on their best behavior and being somebody they really were not.

People often stay in relationships because it feels good, regardless of whether or not they are a good fit for each other. **But time is always going on. If you don't pay attention to the signs God sends you, you might miss "*the one*" that He put on this earth just for you.**

Had I not created and used my list, I could have ended up with this police officer who wined and dined me but didn't necessarily take the time to get to know me. By referencing my list and paying attention to the signs, I was able to give him what I call the "Big X," which freed me to be available for my soulmate. He recognized it before I did, but it never comes how you think it will.

I was helping this gentleman after his wife left him and their two children, and I knew what he needed to work through because of what I had gone through during my first marriage. My experiences helped me help him.

. . .

ALL IN DIVINE ORDER

WE MET AT A CONFERENCE – a personal growth boot camp in Atlanta – when we were both still married. At the time, I was starting a travel business in Maryland that he helped me grow. We were just friendly colleagues, and neither of us knew what was going on in the other's personal life.

At our third or fourth conference, a year after my first marriage was finally over, we were walking around the parking lot, chatting as usual after a big lunch. He had never said anything about what was going on with his marriage, but it came out that day at the end of the conference. When I heard what he was going through, I remember looking up, shaking my head, and thinking, "WOW, Lord! Now I know why you had me go through what I went through last December!"

I was able to help him only because of what I had gone through. **All in Divine Order! God had us meet like this, and He made me go through everything I'd been through for a reason. I realized then that it wasn't by accident that we met.**

I'VE BEEN through a lot in my life, especially in terms of health. I was diagnosed with sarcoidosis in 1989, and because of the medicine they treated the sarcoidosis with, I had to have five different hip surgeries. The first one was when I was twenty-six, a few months after my son was born. Before the surgery, I couldn't walk, and I couldn't trust myself to carry my new bundle of joy without falling. They told me it would get better after I had my son and lost weight, but that didn't happen.

The first surgery on my left hip worked out well. However, my right hip broke down a year later. The same doctor did the surgery, and everything was good upfront, but it didn't last. Because these replacements are artificial materials in your body, they usually only last about ten to fifteen years. I had to go back the following year and have that right hip done all over again, which wasn't normal.

There were times during those five surgeries that I would stand up and not be sure if either of my legs were going to carry me. I understood at twenty-six years old what it was like not to be able to walk for six or seven weeks – to not be able to move your leg from the bed, drop it on the floor and pick it back up again.

God puts us through these things for a reason. Having those hip surgeries helped me to empathize with others, such as seniors and those with disabilities, as I understood what they go through. It helped me not only to truly appreciate the small things (walking, running, bending to pick up something from the floor), which I call blessings, but also to not take them for granted as most people do.

When I had another hip surgery in 2009, I declared that it would be my last one. "Lord, I am too old for hip surgeries." Since then, I had been keeping my weight down and taking supplements.

One day, while preparing for our family photo at Gee-Gee's house, I went to pick up my youngest grandson. When I put him down, something happened in my back. I had to pull out my fold-up cane, as I couldn't walk, and I ended up at the hospital emergency room, thinking that it was my hip, even though I'd never felt that way before.

They found out that I had a herniated disc, which was hitting my nerve and causing shooting pains down my right leg. It would come and go, but when it came, it was excruciating! That year, 2013, the company I was working with had lots of great training sessions, and I was building a team of professional credit agents. Nobody knew that I wasn't going to be at the training sessions, until the day came when they showed up and I didn't.

Luckily, I was able to plug people into the system from my bed and won a lot of awards for all of the people I'd helped and all of the things I'd accomplished. I was just amazed and thanking God for that, laughing at the irony of what had happened. I said that I was never going to have another hip surgery; instead, I got a herniated disc, resulting in surgery. I learned that I have to be more specific in what I ask for!

I want you to remember that there's hope for everybody, regardless of where or who you are – everyone has the talent and ability to get to the next level and joyfully find happiness. All in Divine Order!

REFLECTION QUESTIONS

1. Looking back on your life, were there signs that you missed at the time that now seem so obvious?

2. Have you learned to look for those small signs, or do you still miss them?

3. Sometimes, pain is the ultimate teacher. Have you been through hard experiences that gave you wisdom and made you stronger?

4. Have you noticed that people who struggle come out on the other side stronger than those who have never struggled?

5. Have you found empathy for another person's pain after experiencing some of your own?

6. What was the hardest moment in your life? What did you learn from that experience?

7. If you could go back in time and remove those hard moments from your life, would you still be the same person you are today?

ACTIVITIES

Look back on your past moments of pain. Are there losses from which you haven't yet fully healed? Are you still living in reference to a lost relationship or lost job? Make a breakup list and include everything you loved and hated about it. Better yet, start your Relationship List with all three columns: **Must Have, Must NOT Have, Can Bend.**

Note: you can build these reference lists for any relationship: personal, job, intimate, etc.

Take a look at how your life has changed since those difficult experiences and focus on ways in which you can move forward and cut ties with the bonds of the past. Find a path to your own freedom. It's healthy and natural to grieve a lost relationship, but it's also healthy to say goodbye. Always remember that when God closes one door, He always opens a much better door.

CHAPTER 3 - GRANDMA HELEN

Therefore I say unto you, whatever things you ask when you pray, believe that you receive them, and you will have them.
– Mark 11:24 NKJV

I MENTIONED GEE-GEE, my maternal grandmother, earlier in the book. Grandma Helen was my paternal grandmother. She only had one child, my father, who she had out of wedlock in 1941. Back in that time, such a situation was shunned by the community, so my grandmother Helen and my great-grandmother Ida, affectionately called Grandma Ida, lived together for all their lives.

Grandma Helen worked around the clock as a private duty nurse, going from one job to another. She took it upon herself to make money for her family because her father told her on his death bed, "Helen, take care of your mother. She's not good with money, and she needs you."

She took that seriously. Grandma Ida had eleven children, my grandmother being her second child and oldest daughter. My father was raised as one of

Grandma Ida's children because she was married while Grandma Helen wasn't.

Grandma Helen loved us dearly. After my father died, one of the things I'll never forget her saying is, "You never expect to outlive your children."

Losing her only son was really hard on her. She wanted to keep him on life support, but that was not what he wanted. His wife at the time, my stepmother, had to make a hard decision. She pulled us all together before talking to the medical team, but she ultimately had to go against my grandmother's wishes.

My mother and I didn't get along, so I went to live with Grandma Helen when I was sixteen. Grandma Helen was the type that would complain about things but really didn't want them fixed. The thing she would complain about the most was her siblings. There was always at least one sibling living with her and Grandma Ida at any given time, as her house had enough extra rooms for several people to come live with her.

One day, after hearing Grandma Helen complaining about my uncle, I bucked up against him, and we ended up getting into a physical altercation. I was a lot younger than he was, but he was acting incredibly rude, and I hated that. Of course, this upset Grandma Helen even more because she never liked confrontation; she just liked to complain about things.

That was a real wake-up call for me. I realized that people complain about things in and out. They're not trying to figure out a solution to fix them; they just want to complain about them, whereas I, the problem solver, am always thinking, "What can we do about it? How can we make this better?"

This is what I said to my husband's first wife: "I can't stop you from acting as you do or from talking about me, but I *can* stop you from doing it 'in my backyard.' Meaning, you will not come here and act with disrespect to me or anyone else."

People will talk about us when we're not around. But why should it matter? How does complaining help with whatever it is that we're supposed to be doing and moving into our purpose? Let me just say that it doesn't help at all; complaining actually stifles your purpose.

My life experiences have taught me to advance and not get caught up in "traffic." That's the point of divine order: we don't always have control over a situation, but we do have control over our choices. Take that control and be an action-taker – a problem solver. Others can help you do better if you want to, but if you don't truly want to do better, nothing is going to change.

REFLECTION QUESTIONS

1. Have you spent too long focusing on problems that are outside of your control to fix?

2. Have you been distracted by all of the "traffic"?

3. Are there people in your life who are distracting or have distracted you with their words and actions?

4. How can you stop things outside of your control from affecting your emotional state?

5. Do you find yourself spending a lot of time complaining instead of taking action and solving problems?

6. Do you ever complain purely because you hope that someone else will solve the problem or the problem will just disappear? Has complaining ever solved that problem?

7. Do you think that complaining while being re-

luctant to take action can be beneficial in any situation?

Activities

There are some things in life that you can control and some that you can't. Often, the television we watch and the radio we listen to fill us with stress about issues outside of our control. Do you have influences in your life that are stressing you out rather than entertaining you and making you feel better?

Open up your journal and create two columns: "**things I can control**" and "**things outside of my control.**" Write down everything in your life that makes your life worse, increases your stress, or just bothers you. Divide what you've written down into the things that you can control and things that you can't.

From there, make a plan on how to diminish the influence of those things that you cannot control, as well as a plan of action to improve the things that you can control.

CHAPTER 4 - DADDY

And whatever you do in word or deed, do all in the name of the Lord Jesus, giving thanks to God the Father through Him.
– Colossians 3:17 NKJV

I DIDN'T KNOW what cancer was when my father was diagnosed in 1979. I was in eighth grade. He was given six months but lived until 1988. I was close with my stepmother, and even after he was gone, we would keep in touch. I would visit her and help her around the house, and she gave me a lot of information on what he had gone through in his final years.

Because he changed his diet, he lived significantly longer. He would drink carrot and chlorophyll juice, which he or someone who loved him would juice every day, and he cut all of the sugars, white flour, and refined foods from his diet. Those changes helped him live for another nine years.

He was in and out of the hospital toward the end. I remember that he had a tube down his nose to help him breathe, and he used to squeeze our hands, once for yes and two for no, so that we could talk and communicate with him.

When he could still write, he wrote a note on some paper for me to give to my mother because they had separated when I was eight. He wrote, "Tell your mother it's time to make peace; tell her to come see me." I don't know if he was even conscious at that time, but my mother came, and they made peace.

May 1988 is when he died – the same month I bought my first house after graduating. He never got to see the house. I remember that we would go to the hospital and see him getting worse, responding less and less as the days went on. I even remember thinking, "If he's going to die, just go ahead and die."

The night before he died, I had a dream. We all came in to see him, and my stepmother sat us down and said that we had to decide if we still wanted to have him resuscitated. She talked to us to get our opinion first before she told the doctors not to. Before we left, we went to see him. When we got to his room, I was the last one to enter as I saw him standing outside the door, and he was young. He told me, "I want to talk to you." As everyone else entered where he lay in the bed, he and I stayed behind. He told me that he was fine, that he was going to be okay and that he wanted me not to worry about him. Everything was going to be fine, and everything would be taken care of.

I shared my dream with my stepmother, and she said that it wasn't a dream. That was him coming to me to let me know that he was going to be okay and that he was getting ready to transition over. It made sense to me – that was something Daddy would do.

My grandmother had my father out of wedlock, but his name was the same name as my grandfather, his father. I only got to know my paternal grandfather later on as an adult. He dated the woman that lived two houses away from my first house, and he would come by often. I just didn't know that it was him.

He married somebody else before I was born. He had two sons, and his first son was also named after him, giving him two sons with the same name. One of the things that my father was very sensitive about was being a bastard. There was a lot that he dealt with and overcame, and I see where I get a lot of my thought process. My mother used to tell me that I never accepted things – I always had to ask questions like a rebel, and that's what my father did, too.

My father didn't do any chemo; he just changed his diet and lived nine years instead of the six months he was given. Doing what other people tell you to do is never your only option – even if those people are doctors, nurses, or specialists. You can decide to take a holistic approach. It's extra work, but it's worth managing your life. After all, who do you think cares more – you or the doctors? I always say, use professionals as encyclopedias. Remember, they get paid regardless of your outcome.

We were made the way we are for a reason. Embracing "all in divine order" means accepting that we are part of something bigger. Always pay attention, think, and ask; regardless of what people say, keep asking. That's how we got to the moon. Don't let anybody stop you from looking deeper and deciding for yourself. Remember to consult the true authority, your Creator the Most High.

Reflection Questions

1. Do you see yourself as part of a larger plan or the result of something random?

2. Does being part of a larger plan give you a better sense of significance?

3. Does seeing yourself as insignificant affect your self-confidence and how you view yourself?

4. How can you increase your faith in yourself?

5. Have you allowed other people to stop you from following your dreams?

6. Do you have regrets in life that came from listening to other people?

7. Have you ever surrendered to something without questioning it, even though you could have sought a different path?

Activities

Take a look at the times in your life when things got tough. Have there been moments when you've made decisions based on incorrect information? Have you been guided by advice from people who weren't qualified?

Make a conscious choice to do the research before you make your next major life decision. Create a system where you write down the pros and cons in your journal. This is a safe place where you can reflect in private. Don't take things at face value; instead, allow ideas to percolate for a few days before you make decisions. And always remember to ask your Higher Power, as I always do. Mine is God. Who or what is yours?

CHAPTER 5 - MENTORS FOR A REASON, A SEASON, A LIFETIME

For the love of money is a root of all kinds of evil, for which some have strayed from the faith in their greediness, and pierced themselves through with many sorrows.
– 1 Timothy 6:10 NKJV

I MET this guy when I worked in a travel network marketing company. You see, tax laws are designed for business owners, not for employees. I always said after I had my first job that everyone needs to file a schedule C, meaning that you should have a home-based business or a side business to maximize your hard-earned money.

When I first started in network marketing, I wasn't doing it to make money. People would tell me, "You can get rich doing this," but that was never my intention. It was just to be able to buy what I wanted and keep more money in my pocket from my well-paying, W2 wage-earner job.

This gentleman had a training platform with various network marketing training sessions, my favorite being called "Communications Mastery," which was all about personality types, including knowing your particular personality type and identifying other types. When you know who you are, how you act, and why you act the way you do, only then can you begin to understand others and, more importantly, know how to interact with those who are unlike you.

Because I'm big on personal development, I stuck with him and, for a season, called him my mentor. **Formal education is purposefully designed to give us what we need to be an employee and stay in the rat race on that hamster wheel – but it doesn't give us what we need for personal development to do greater and move into purpose. Pay attention to those who are put in your path for a reason, a season, or a lifetime to give you what you need to manifest your purpose.**

Since I was a season pass holder, I was invited to a special training session that he was doing in New Jersey, just a couple of hours from where I lived. Two of my colleagues and I went to this training a couple of times, and we began taking groups of people with us. At first, we weren't expecting to do anything other than attend a seminar, but he asked us a crucial question: how many people did we know with less-than-perfect credit?

I knew several people who needed their credit fixed, including me, so we ended up getting started with that particular company for which he was training. We went to the first convention in Atlanta in 2010, and it felt like, "Wow, we've got something here!" We met the owners and other senior staff members at the convention and decided that it was something into which we could plant our feet to make a difference and help lots of people.

We were part of a group of less than seventy to kick off the YFL Foundation, a nonprofit to educate youth on matters of personal finance, which included a scholarship program. The first time, we gave $25,000 in scholarships. Today, we open it up every fall to give away over $400,000 to high school seniors and college freshmen. This is the same company where I received all of those awards, even though I was stuck in bed. When I was introduced to it, my husband encouraged me to stick with it, and it started overtaking my insurance business.

One of the things that Divine Order does is show people how to build their own bank through the proper life insurance designed specifically to borrow from when you need funds and pay yourself back in a way that won't affect your credit if you miss a payment.

My good friend died last year, and her children, who were in their mid-twenties, were still living in the house with her. She left them a good amount of money through insurance, and they were able to pay off the house and get it remodeled. I was able to assist and help them set up the proper asset protection entities and vehicles to pay them in the future.

My father, being an "outside the box" thinker, set things up so that we would have a trust. He was on the right track, but he didn't know that he had to actually set the trust up before he died. He thought it could be set up afterward or that it was already set up by what he had put in place before he died.

Unfortunately, everything that wasn't insurance went into probate and his estate, which was probated, as well. Obviously, this was not his plan, and since he wasn't around people who operated in this space, he didn't have anyone to accurately direct him in accomplishing the legacy he'd attempted to build and leave behind.

When youth who lose their parent(s) are left large amounts of money, it's not always the best idea for them to access that money. **They're grieving from the loss of a loved one and given all of this money in one lump sum. Most people would blow a good chunk of it, and rightly so, in their mourning, but they still have to live after that. They need to have something that they can survive off of as they move through the mourning process.**

Please be responsible and do your due diligence on finding someone who knows how to set up your assets in such a way that your plan is carried out for your family, and they don't end up blowing their entire fortune. If you're unable to identify anyone, feel free to reach out to us at www.divineordernetwork.com. We help to set people and families up before they find themselves in the midst of a demise. Having a working, bulletproof system into which to plug your family is key.

Here's something my mentor put in place for his business and taught me to do for mine. Team building is all about having something that's duplicable; it's about making money when you're not working. You do the work upfront and put things in place so that if something comes up, you can walk away, and your team is still working and growing. I've learned that this applies not only to network marketing but also leaving a legacy for your family.

One of the lessons that I have learned is not to rely too much on an outside entity to take my team or my family to where it needs to be. Once you learn something, you should always document it and be prepared to show it to others. A duplicable system is

essential to growing, nurturing, and consistently engaging a success team.

Jesus, known to many as the first team builder, started with a team of twelve when He was alive. Shortly after His death, burial, and resurrection, about three thousand were added to that team (Acts 2:41). Today, the estimated count is about 2.4 billion Christians, according to worldpopulation.com!

Reflection Questions

1. How do you see formal education? Does a degree instantly make a person wiser?
2. Have you met people who had great success despite a lack of formal education?
3. Have you let your lack of education hold you back from jobs and projects that you know you could handle?
4. Have you ever wanted to venture out on your own but have been too afraid to take that first step?
5. Have you relied on others, even when you had what you needed inside of you the entire time?
6. Has the fear of the unknown or fear of failure ever held you back?
7. Have you ever left something half-done, and then regretted not completing it?

Activities

In order to achieve true financial freedom and put real money in your pocket, you have to aim at making money even when you're not working. Separating the connection between time and income is the first step on the path to financial freedom. Education teaches us to trade time for dollars, but there is a better way!

Make a list of all of your business ideas in your journal. Do any of them sever the connection between time and money? Does one of them stand out from the rest? Look for opportunities where you can be paid for the same work more than once. Write them down in your journal and turn your best idea into a plan of action.

CHAPTER 6 - APOLLO THE DOG

To everything there is a season, A time for every purpose under heaven: A time to be born, and a time to die; A time to plant, and a time to pluck what is planted; A time to kill, and a time to heal; A time to break down, and a time to build up; A time to weep, and a time to laugh; A time to mourn, and a time to dance; A time to cast away stones, and a time to gather stones; A time to embrace, and a time to refrain from embracing; a time to gain, and a time to lose; a time to keep, and a time to throw away; a time to tear, and a time to sew; a time to keep silence, and a time to speak; A time to love, and a time to hate; a time of war, and a time of peace
– Ecclesiastes 3:1-8 NKJV

APOLLO WAS A TWELVE-YEAR-OLD POODLE. I didn't even want a dog; you get stuck with the responsibility, not to mention the fact that I am allergic to them. But my son had been growing up by himself. He was going through some struggles, and his daddy thought that we should get a dog to help him. But I ended up having to raise this dog.

I then got confirmation that he had carcinoma –

cancer in his chest cavity. He would cough from time to time, and it sounded like an adult human with emphysema. The first time I heard this deep cough through the night, I took him to the vet. They did their tests and sent me to another doctor. When I took him to the specialist, he didn't cough at all, so they didn't hear it. All of that testing ended up being $1600. Throughout this process, I kept my son and my first husband in the loop, hoping that they might pitch in. After all, I didn't want a dog in the first place!

When the doctor called me, he told me that Apollo had a couple of weeks left to live. I looked online and tried to learn what I could. After the experience with my father, I was into doing this holistically instead of doing chemotherapy and radiation. I believe that **we should always try to learn from our experiences so that we can stop them from happening or make them happen more frequently – whatever it is that we need.**

During my research, I found out about the Myer cocktail. Dr. John Myer created a cocktail where they put vitamins through the body intravenously. When I asked about it, they said that they don't do that anymore and gave me another appointment a week later.

I called a holistic doctor, and they told me about a procedure where they draw blood out of your neck, insert oxygen into the blood, and put it back into the body so that it can kill the cancer cells. You're supposed to have several of those treatments roughly every three weeks for it to work.

During the hour-long drive to have this procedure done, I called my first husband, who bought the dog. He said, "It's good that you have him, because I know I couldn't have done it. If it was $1,600, it wouldn't have been done."

Once you commit to something that can't take care of itself, it's a commitment. You have to deal with it.

That's one thing for which I had been praying. I said, "Okay, Lord. I know there's a reason for this." I kept asking myself, "How did he get this?" The holistic doctor told me that it was probably due to his diet, proceeding to inform me that the dry dog food process was documented to carry carcinogens. I had been feeding him expensive prescription dog food, and it really hit me hard because I felt like I had done this to him.

Some people would just put him to sleep, but that's not who I am, and I knew I couldn't do it. I just asked God to guide me through it all. I knew that Apollo was not feeling well, but he was still spunky; he still wanted to go on walks with me, and that's why I kept working with him.

By that point, he was on raw food and drinking alkaline water. We were both drinking it, and I had even hoped to bathe in it soon. That small change was really making a difference. Thanks to Apollo, I learned so many things I had no clue of before.

Divine Order always manifests itself and will eventually show you why you go through tough situations.

Apollo was a fighter. Even though he was a miniature poodle, he had a strong will, and I learned so much from this experience. The entire time I researched, I felt like it was for a reason. Everything I learned was something that might one day be needed, whether it be for a family member or me, because cancer is very common, especially in our family. I just wanted to make sure that I was doing what I was supposed to.

The bible tells us that we all have an appointed time to leave this earth, and only God knows when that is. I kept asking God why He wanted me to make this decision for Apollo. I'd pray, "Please don't make me decide. Isn't that supposed to be Your decision, LORD?" Well, I guess not for dogs, huh?

God put the decision on my heart the weekend following Thanksgiving, after paying to have fluid drained from Apollo's lungs against the doctor's advice. I thought, "Perhaps I'd euthanize Apollo when my father-in-law dies." We had no idea when that might be, but he was in a nursing home and not doing well at all.

On the morning of November 28, 2017, the Tuesday following Thanksgiving, I got the text that my father-in-law had passed during the night, and I called the animal hospital to arrange Apollo's transition.

That was one of the hardest things that I have ever had to do. I truly don't like "playing God" and wanted to leave these types of decisions up to Him. I still have recurring memories of the feeling of Apollo dropping limply in my arms...steadily confirming why I didn't even really want a dog, all while cherishing the memories and love that he had provided for so many. This was so heavy on my heart that I wrote a book called *Apollo's Story* in the hopes of comforting owners, young and old, who find themselves having to "play God" with their beloved pets.

REFLECTION QUESTIONS

1. Take a moment to look at your life right now. Is there a sign that you are missing?

2. Have you had moments in your life where it took

progressively bigger hints to guide you toward the right decision?

3. Have you had a scary moment in your life where you thought your number was up? How did you move forward?

4. What does commitment mean to you?

5. Have you had commitments that turned out to require more than you expected?

6. Have you ever let somebody down by committing to something and not doing it? How did that make you feel?

7. Have you ever realized only after the fact why certain things were happening to you? Were you able to apply that knowledge and wisdom to the present moment?

ACTIVITIES

Continue to reflect on the course of your life. Try to find the waypoints that led you to where you are today. Are there lessons that you could have learned earlier? Were there small decisions that turned into something larger? Looking at the path of your life, can you start to see a Divine Order that brought you to where you are today?

Where is Divine Order taking your life? What is your vision and path for the future? Write it down and track your journey in your journal.

CHAPTER 7 - PARTNERS IN SHINE

*L**et your light so shine before men, that they may see your good works and glorify your Father in heaven.*
Matthew 5:16 (NKJV)

GOD PUT TOGETHER Divine Order and Divine Order Network, which sponsored the "Leonet and Monica – Partners in Shine" radio show. Our goal is to shine peace, love, harmony, light, and positivity on each and every person with whom we come in contact, and that's why they call us Partners in Shine!! Although we often talk about putting money back into people's pockets, our vision is to change people's mindsets and provide the necessary tools for their transition to abundance.

This vision came about as we were growing our team. Leonet and I were talking one day and had some great conversations that we realized people needed to hear. I said, "This might be time for a radio show!" But we needed a name for the show.

Both of us have often been called "Sunshine," and people often say, "You come in with a shine," because we have such positive attitudes and are very upbeat. People would also call us "partners in crime," but I never liked that. It just didn't fit. But God put on my heart the title, "Partners in Shine," and the name just stuck.

It is a choice to let your light shine, regardless of what's going on, how you feel, or what spirnancial pain you might be experiencing, whether it's spiritual, mental, emotional, physical, social, or financial. When we walk by someone and say hello with a smile, it's a decision that we make every time; we have control over it.

There are a couple of instances that are perfect examples of this. I was once walking into a store, and a gentleman was walking toward me. I was just walking and smiling, just doing what I do. He comes up and says, "Nice smile. I think I'll pass it on!" That was really cool, and you never know who you can affect positively.

Another time, Leonet and I were traveling together for the first time for a training session in Atlanta. As we were walking to a restaurant and chatting, someone was walking toward us. As I normally do, I smiled and said, "Hello, how are you doing?" and we just kept walking. Leonet said, "You realize they didn't speak to you," and she gave me a funny look.

I said, "I don't care whether they speak to me or not. I did my part. I don't give to get back. I give because that's what we are supposed to do. I did what I know God wants me to do." That was a wake-up call for her, and that's when people started calling her Sunshine, as well.

Reflection Questions

1. Have you ever felt good because of a kind word or a smile from a stranger?

2. Have you ever smiled at a stranger yourself?

3. Does the thought of being a part of something larger and being able to make a difference with a smile excite you and make you feel good?

4. Would you like to surround yourself with people who are on the same journey as you?

5. How can you affect the world in a meaningful way?

6. How can you turn your dreams into reality?

7. Would you like to surround yourself with people who can help you find the answers to these questions?

Activities

It's time to unlock Your Purpose in life. In your journal, dig deep and write down your life definition. What is your purpose on this planet? Are you doing everything you can to make the world a better place for the people around you?

Why are you here, and what are you doing with your opportunities? How can you start to do better? Are you ready to tap into your own Divine Order? It's time for you to find a way to shine.

CALL TO ACTION

We encourage you to make the choice to shine peace, love, harmony, light, and positivity on each and every person with whom you come in contact. We'd love to assist you in finding your purpose, as well as working in your purpose all in Divine Order.

If you'd like to join our movement, follow the links below:

Spirnancial Partners in Shine
Like our FB page: @SpirnancialPNS
Join the private FB group:
https://www.facebook.com/groups/412746286083478/

Divine Order Network
Like the **Divine Order Network** FB Page:
@divineordernetwork

Subscribe to our YouTube Channel,
Divine Order Network

Check Our Website:
www.divineordernetwork.com
You can schedule an appointment, look closer at

how we can help you and your family put money back in your pockets, donate to the Divine Order Foundation, or inquire about the Gee-Gee Scholarship fund.

Welcome to our Spirnancial Partner in Shine Family!

We're very excited about you moving and being in Your Purpose... All in Divine Order 💚

Allow me to share other Scriptures that help me stay Spirnancially Balanced in Divine Order.

Give ear to my words, O LORD, Consider my meditation. Give heed to the voice of my cry, My King and my God, For to You I will pray. My voice You shall hear in the morning, O LORD; In the morning I will direct it to You, And I will look up. (Psalms 5:1-3 NKJV)

Be anxious for nothing, but in everything by prayer and supplication, with thanksgiving, let your requests be made known to God; and the peace of God, which surpasses all understanding, will guard your hearts and minds through Christ Jesus. (Philippians 4:6-7 NKJV)

For God has not given us a spirit of fear, but of power and of love and of a sound mind. (2 Timothy 1:7 NKJV)

Trust in the LORD with all your heart and lean not on your own understanding; In all your ways acknowledge Him, and He shall direct your paths. (Proverbs 3:5-6)

ABOUT THE AUTHOR

Chaplain Dr. Monica Young Andrews, the oldest of three, grew up in the District of Columbia, America's national capital. She attended catholic school and is a proud Hampton University alumnus. Although her background is in computer science, she's been in the financial arena for over ten years and has always been a practicing advocate of the application of knowledge. At age fifteen, after receiving her first paycheck, she quickly learned about "Uncle Sam" but didn't understand why he was taking so much of her money, since she didn't even have an uncle named Sam!

Since 2010, she has worked fervently to equip thousands with the knowledge, tools and resources necessary to create everlasting wealth for true legacy building. She realized long ago that if she can ask ten people a question to which at least 80 percent know the answer, then why does she need to retain that information? Instead, she needs to know what those ten people do not. She has thus spent decades learning and practicing what the average person doesn't know. This may come in the form of credit repair and restoration, asset protection, tax benefits, the infinite banking concept, personal and business credit worthiness, day-to-day best practices, business funding, franchising, and book writing.

Because of her recognized contributions over the last twenty-plus years, she was respectfully nominated to receive her honorary doctorate from Global Oved Dei Seminary (GODSU) in 2016. Those contributions include her other books, *RESPECT: What Does It Mean To You?*, a book for teenagers, parents or anyone who has ever felt disrespected, and *Apollo's Story*. *Apollo's Story*, written as a way to heal from the traumatic decision she had to make for her puppy, aims to prayerfully heal other pet owners and their families as they struggle with the decision to euthanize their beloved pets.

Dr. Andrews' other contributions include Divine Order, which supports the Divine Order Network and Spirnancial Partners in Shine movements, as well as the Divine Order Foundation. She has put together these foundations to elevate the Spirnancial well-being of humanity, one person, family, community and company at a time, through education, tools and experience. Dr. Andrews is a true example of a "real teacher" defined in the book *Fake* by the infamous Mr. Robert Kiyosaki, author of *Rich Dad, Poor Dad*.

Chaplain Dr. Monica Andrews enjoys spending time with her family, traveling and making a difference wherever God leads her.

Prayerfully, you'll join the Divine Order movement!

*"Knowledge is power; however,
the APPLICATION of knowledge makes you
POWERFUL."*
– Chaplain Dr. Monica Young Andrews

Continue to move full of POWER 💡

www.ingramcontent.com/pod-product-compliance
Lightning Source LLC
Chambersburg PA
CBHW071322080526
44587CB00018B/3321